IMAGES
of Wales

AROUND
NEATH

To Norman

with Best wishes

Best Wishy

in Friendship + Esteem

An old blast furnace, Neath Abbey, *c.* 1960 (see p. 74 for full details).

IMAGES
of Wales

AROUND
NEATH

Compiled by
Stephen Absalom and Robert King

TEMPUS

First published 1998
Reprinted 2000
Copyright © Stephen Absalom and Robert King, 1998

Tempus Publishing Limited
The Mill, Brimscombe Port,
Stroud, Gloucestershire, GL5 2QG

ISBN 0 7524 1149 7

Typesetting and origination by
Tempus Publishing Limited
Printed in Great Britain by
Midway Clark Printing, Wiltshire

Careg Bica is a fine example of a standing stone, measuring a very imposing ten feet tall, and is located on Y Mynydd Drummau. Like all monoliths, we cannot be sure about the reason for their existence, or their purpose. One legend has it that Careg Bica goes down to the River Neath on Easter morning for a drink of water. One strange fact described by Chris Torrance, the Vale of Neath poet, was that if you strip to your waist on a very cold day, and lay against the stone with the wind biting into you, you will feel a heat travel through your body. Try it, I have. It is true. For many years after the Second World War, there was an annual cricket match played near the stone. At Easter two teams from Skewen would fight it out. Sadly the match no longer takes place.

Contents

Stephen Absalom and Robert King

Acknowledgements

We would like to thank the following for supplying pictures and information:
Bill Absalom, Jessie Adams, Lilian Adams, Winifred Alexander, David Allen, Mr Allin, Miriam Bailey, Alan Bater, Don Bater, Thomas Branch, Roy Clement, Mary Collins, Alan Copp, Mr and Mrs Don Davies, Mary Davies, Christina Duncan, Mrs G. Ebbage, Reg Elias, Eurof Evans, Griffith Evans, Waine Foster, David Fox, Freda Gibbins, Wayne Gitus, E.W. Griffiths, Phyllis Griffiths, Alec Hayward, Huw James, John A. Jenkins, Dan Jones, Ronald Jones, Tom Jones, Tom J. Jones, E.M. King, Margaret King, David Kreischer, Cllr Moria Lewis, Dr Brian Loosmore, Mark Matthews, Mrs H. McNeil, Elizabeth Mort, Val Payne, Hilda Peters, Mrs Walter Price, Ivor Roberts, Wyndam Roch, John Rosser, Murial Rowley, Mrs Russen, Dennis Shepherd, Ronald James Smith, Hubert Speight, Percy Thomas, Clive Trott, Kate Walters Keith Wathan, Beryl Williams, Mrs M. Willings, and to Raymond Wilson, for the pictures on pp. 86 and 87.

Introduction

The photographs included in this book come from our personal collections which have been built up over the past thirty years. We hope that they will enhance an understanding of the industrial and cultural change that Neath has seen this century.

The book will take you to the big houses of Neath, which have fallen into disrepair and ultimate obscurity. Barren land or housing estates have now replaced these sites. Such is the case with Cwrt Herbert. This Abbey Grange had a chequered history before its demolition, playing host to people like Rees Gronow, who is mentioned in literature's 'Who's Who'; and the laureate Robert Southey who passed time there in 1801. Southey fell in love with the Vale of Neath and although he came to reside in Keswick, he often referred with regret to the fact that his home was not in Dyffryn Nedd.

In Neath we rightly hold the ironmaster, Joseph Tregelles Price, in high esteem. He was a philanthropist and Quaker and was well known for his conscience about the working classes. He fought hard for a reprieve for Dic Penderyn who was hanged in Cardiff for his part in the Merthyr Uprising. He was ultimately unsuccessful, although his letters and petitions on the subject live to this day. Unlike his peers, he considered Penderyn to be innocent. Price lies in the Quaker graveyard in James Street. We have included the cover of a pamphlet on these pages which epitomizes the way posterity considers him.

The book will take a tour of Neath, from the Mackworth's of the Gnoll, to the real people of Neath who worked and laboured for their families. It will travel from monoliths like Carreg Bica high on the Drummau, to the ships that still frequent the mouth of the Nedd with their deliveries of sand and coal. It is the contrasting scenes of the town that have always delighted us.

Although Neath is not often thought of as a coastal town, the borough has a beach at Jersey Marine which was, if only locally in pre-private car times, a Mecca for Sunday school trips and glorious days out before the Great War. The tower contained, in its heyday, a camera obscura. Jersey Marine today is a sleepy village with a deserted beach used only by walkers and horse riders. The Vale of Neath is well known for its natural beauty from Aberdulais to Pontneddfechan, to the waterfalls and rivers which are fed by the wild Beacons. The meandering River Nedd gathers in power as it runs down the valley to Briton Ferry, to eventually drain into the Bristol Channel. It was at Neath Abbey that industry built the first iron boat, under the watchful eye of the ruins built by long-dead monks. Sailors loaded coal and iron from its wharves and travelled the nineteenth-century world.

Romance and superstition remain, and it is not hard to realize why. Walk along the needle-thread turnpikes at night and be overwhelmed by recollections of stories about horsemen calling at The Stag in Abergarwed, knocking the lantern light and shouting. The horsemen would always be dressed in black. Do they still frequent Cwm Nedd today? Walk the night road and you might believe they do.

We have acknowledged the owners of pictures we have used and stored down the years, although some of these people have unfortunately passed on. Finally, we extend our apologies to anyone we have inadvertently omitted.

Stephen Absalom and Robert King
Abergarwed 1998

Joseph Edward Moore-Gwyn of Longford Court was born Joseph Edward Moore, at Buckland in 1850. He was the eldest son of the Revd Joseph Moore, who was vicar and rural dean at Buckland in Berkshire. His father's sister was Mrs Howel Gwyn. On 6 September 1900, he assumed, by Royal licence, the additional name and arms of Gwyn, in compliance with the will of Howel Gwyn. He also succeeded to the Gwyn's estates at Dyffryn and Abercraf and followed his uncle in maintaining the prestige of this ancient Breconshire family and in enhancing their reputation for usefulness in public life. He was educated at Winchester College, and was married, in 1876, to Edith Rotheringham, eldest daughter of the Revd W. Jephson, rector of Hinton, Berkshire. He served Breconshire as a county councillor, deputy lieutenant, magistrate, and was High Sheriff in 1902. He also served as a magistrate in Glamorgan. He was a staunch churchman with a strong attachment to St Matthew's, Dyffryn, where he served as the vicar's warden for thirty-four years. He had great enthusiasm for both cricket and rugby, with his name appearing among those present at the first meeting of the committee of Glamorgan cricket club which was convened in the Angel Inn, Cardiff in July 1888. In 1899, he is recorded as being president of Neath's football club and athletic association, which also arranged the cricket fixtures at this time. In 1903 he is reported to have been the captain of the first XI. Joseph Edward Moore-Gwyn was succeeded by two sons, Joseph Gwyn and Howel Gwyn, and three daughters.

One
Scenes of Neath

The dorter sub-vault, inside the ruins of the Neath Abbey.

The ruins of Neath Abbey, *c.* 1880.

The Gatehouse, Neath Abbey.

Neath Castle, *c.* 1830.

Ivy Tower, Tonnau, was a folly constructed by the Mackworth family in the eighteenth century, but was damaged by fire at the beginning of the 1900s. The local authority now have plans to re-build it.

Victoria Gardens, c. 1960.

A picturesque winter scene of St David's church, taken from Victoria Gardens.

The town of Neath, seen from the Gnoll grounds, *c.* 1930.

A view of the Dulias Valley village, Crynant, taken from Bryn Bedd, *c.* 1900.

A lovely picture of Cwmclydach dam, with River Clydach running slowly on the left of the path, c. 1956. It was originally built in the mid to late nineteenth century, but is currently being renovated after serious cracks were found in the wall. The building below the dam, in the right of the picture was a cowshed.

Glynfelin House can be seen on the left of this scene, shrouded by trees. To the right is Glynfelin Farm and Drummau Mountain is in the background.

Glynfelin House was damaged during the war. The house was originally built on a site below the waterfall on Cwmclydach in 1780 and was rebuilt on the present site around 1904.

Glynclydach House, c. 1860.

Brick Lodge, Dyffryn Clydach. This was the main entrance to the Gwyn's Dyffryn Mansion.

DYFFRYN MANSION, NEAR NEATH.

This is a gathering in the field below Dyffryn Mansion. Howel Gwyn purchased the Dyffryn Estate from the Williams family, in 1853. In 1854 the mansion was built on an elevated site, in the neo-gothic style. It was constructed of sandstone with Bath stone dressing. The house contained forty-seven rooms including ten principal bedrooms, a billiard room, a library, a smoking room and a servants' hall. There were garages and a stable, which are still in existence today, bearing the date stone 1862. There are also three lodges. The local economic depression in the 1920s eroded the fortunes of many landed families and in 1927 the entire Dyffryn estate was offered for sale. By the early 1930s, the house had been demolished, with some of the stone being used to build the walls of the houses being constructed on Longford Road, Neath Abbey.

Dyffryn Mansion lay empty for many years. The picture opposite shows the local fire service practising fire fighting shortly before the house was demolished, around 1930.

Darren Court, set in the shadow of Drummau Mountain, is arguably the most desirable residence in the area. It was originally built in the early eighteenth century by Elija Waring, who died there in 1857. There is an interesting theory expounded in Rhys Phillip's *History of the Vale of Neath*, regarding the name Darren. In the Ashmole manuscript of 1820 it is stated that, 'There is mention of a "rock called Tarren Dynwyd" in the parish of Llan Gatwg. Probably this is the rock on the eastern face of Mynydd Drummau from which Waring named his Darren House.' The Court stands virtually unchanged and is now owned by the Morgan family.

Cwrt Herbert was one of the Abbey Granges and was home to the Gronows. It is also famous for playing host to the poet Robert Southey in 1801. Rees Gronow sold the property after his father's death, in 1836. Sometime later, it came into the ownership of Sir Griffith Thomas who lived there until he died in 1923. Sir Griffith Thomas, together with his brothers, formed one of the largest shipping companies of anthracite coal in South Wales. He became Mayor of Neath in 1908/9, although, surprisingly, he was not a member of the council. He also served a term, in 1901, as Mayor of Swansea. In latter years, Cwrt Herbert passed to the Price Bros, who were meat merchants and farmers. The building was demolished in the 1960s to make way for a housing estate.

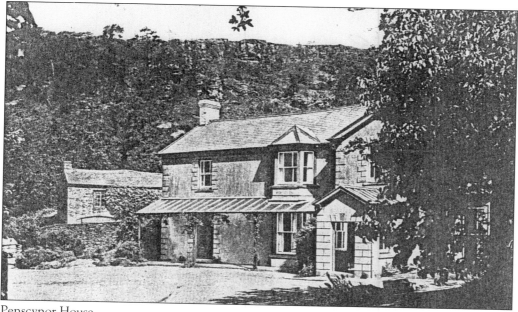

Penscynor House.

Cwrt Rhydhir, at Longford Court was the house of the Moore-Gwyns. It is currently in the ownership of the National Autistic Society.

Ynyslas, Blaengwrach, in the Vale of Neath, was built in the late eighteenth century and owned by the Squire of Aberpergwm. It was demolished in 1960.

Plasnewydd Farm, Bryncoch. This was one of the farms on the Dyffryn Estate which was sold off when the estate was broken up in 1927. It was also called Dyffryn Farm and Home Farm and is now owned by the Thomas family.

Neath Abbey railway station was used as a home for many years before being demolished in the 1980s. The adjoining railway line is now used for mineral haulage only.

Swiss Gables was originally the vicarage of St Matthew's, Dyffryn and was built around 1870.

The picturesque Swiss Cottage, Longford.

Longford Farm.

Penlan Farm, on Drummau Mountain. The farm was last lived in and worked by the Rice family in the 1950s. There is little left now, and the farm has now almost disappeared.

Maes Melyn Farm, Skewen, *c.* 1900.

The cottages in the Cwm, Neath Abbey. The River Clydach meanders on the right.

Cwmclydach Cottages, Dyffryn Clydach.

24

Cottages owned by the ironworks, Neath
Abbey. This row of houses was the home of
John Hopkins, the coal merchant.
Unfortunately, the cottages were left to
decay in the 1920s.

Ty Mawr, Neath Abbey, which was the home of Joseph Tregelles Price.

Glynfelin Lodge was the gateway to Dyffryn, and belonged to the Gibbins family. It is now the home of Donald and Murial Davies, pictured here outside the Lodge with their dog, Henry, in 1979. The Lodge is known locally as the Round House, and is the only thatched dwelling in the area.

The Council school, Crynant, *c.* 1917.

The Gnoll House was originally built for Thomas Evans sometime in the late seventeenth century. However, it is more commonly known as the home of Sir Humphrey Mackworth. The building succeeded to four members of the Mackworth family before being sold in 1811. It then passed into the ownership of several people including Henry Grand Jnr, who was Portreeve of Neath from 1814 to 1829. In 1836 he became the town's first Mayor. The Gnoll House then passed into the ownership of the Neath Corporation, who had the intention of making it a war memorial museum. Several other ideas were passed between the city fathers: such as making it into a college and in the 1920s the idea of a grammar school was mooted. These ideas all came to nothing however, and the house fell into decay and was demolished during a fire fighting exercise in 1956.

Gwyn Hall was given to the town in Howel Gwyn's will. Note his statue pointing to the house across the road where he was born. The statue was ultimately moved to stand in Victoria Gardens. The Gwyn Hall now houses the Neath Muesum.

Neath Abbey Estate office, pictured in the 1950s. In recent years, it has been in the ownership of the Local Education Authority.

The Dyffryn Arms, Bryncoch, *c.* 1912. The duck pond has now gone and the car park, a modern requirement for any public house, has taken its place. The cottage on the left is called Slebech.

Mr and Mrs Tom Davies, to the left and centre, stand with Mrs Morgan, outside Queen's Row, Brynoch, in 1935. The cottages were on a track between Primrose Bank and the Dyffryn Arms, and were demolished in the 1960s.

Onllwyn Inn, in the Dulais Valley was demolished in 1994–5.

The interior of Neath Market, c. 1900. This endearing picture shows the market as it used to be!

The tannery, near the old Neath river bridge, *c.* 1850.

The Onllwyn Welfare Hall, in the 1950s.

A picture of the flooding in Abergarwed taken in the late 1980s.

Mary Laycock and Maude Davies look on in horror, as the hamlet of Abergarwed is flooded. These more recent floods were not so bad as the ones in the 1960s however, one of which cut the villages off for months.

Two
Streets

Orchard Street, *c.* 1950.

Orchard Street, *c*. 1960.

The castle buildings, *c*. 1900.

Skewen public park, *c.* 1932.

The children's playground, in Skewen park, *c.* 1932.

Green Street, *c.* 1950.

Green Street, *c.* 1900.

Cefn-yr-Allt, Aberdulais, *c*. 1930.

Another view of Cefn-yr-Allt, *c*. 1930.

Cefn-yr-Allt, *c.* 1930.

Cilfrew, *c.* 1930.

Penscynor, Cilfrew, *c.* 1930.

This picture of the council houses at Ynysygerwn was taken in 1932. It is little changed today.

Parkfield, Tonnau, *c.* 1930.

A view of Onllwyn in the Dulais Valley.

Another view of Onllwyn in the Dulais Valley.

Jersey Marine village, *c.* 1850.

This point in Skewen is still called White Gates. The picture shows coal from the Skewen Main Colliery being hauled to the Neath Abbey Wharf.

This is where Taillwyd Road joined New Road, Neath Abbey, *c.* 1870.

Neath Abbey village, *c.* 1900. This scene is little changed a hundred years on.

New Road, Skewen, *c*. 1890.

New Road, Skewen, c. 1900.

The Square and Orchard Street, c. 1890.

Stockham's Corner Neath

Stockham's Corner. On January 31 1988, Stockham, the bakery and confectioner firm celebrated its 100th anniversary. It is Neath's oldest bakery and was originally situated on the corner of Windsor Road and Briton Ferry Road. The story of how the bakery came into existence is a fascinating one. It began in Bridgewater, in the 1870s, where William Stockham, a lad of twelve years of age, lived with his family. His father ran a building firm and, as the eldest lad, William was expected to work in the business. He, however, had other ideas and left one night through a bedroom window and walked to Gloucester. Arriving there in the early hours, he saw a light and found it was a bakehouse. They gave him a cup of tea and eventually offered him a job. By the time he was fourteen-years-old, he had risen to become the foreman but again wanderlust was getting the better of him. Through a roundabout route, which took him via Swansea where he found employment in another bakehouse, he heard about similar premises in Neath. It was here that William set up Stockham's as we know it today. He began by renting the building and repairing the ovens during his time off from working in Swansea. When everything was to his satisfaction, he piled all his belongings onto a handcart, and walked to Neath. William continued to work at these premises for forty-five years. From these early beginnings, the business had been handed down through four generations until it closed a few years ago. The author's father, William Henry Absalom, worked at Stockham's as a baker for thirty years, before taking up a single handed bakery at Allin's, a company on the other side of town.

Neath Abbey village, in the 1880s.

Wind Street, *c*. 1930.

Old Road, Skewen, in the 1870s.

Jersey Marine village, *c.* 1938.

The Cwm, Neath Abbey, *c.* 1900. Note the cottage on the right and the viaduct in background.

Neath Abbey, *c.* 1890.

This viaduct crossed over what is locally called Mooretown Hill, Skewen, *c.* 1970.

Stanley Road, Skewen. Note the stack of the Main Colliery in the background.

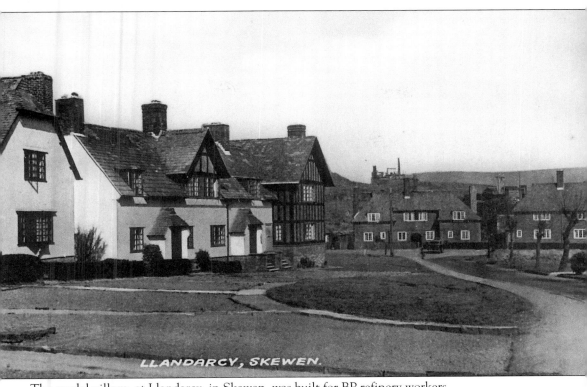

LLANDARCY, SKEWEN.

The model village, at Llandarcy, in Skewen, was built for BP refinery workers.

A Neath gas tram at The Terminus Hotel, Neath Abbey.

Riverside Row, Neath Abbey. The house in foreground was lived in by 'Hopkins the Coal' and the other houses down the row were occupied by the families of Mrs Griffiths, Rewbridge, Blackmore and Jones. At the end of the row was the coal yard. Like all the cottages on the banks of the Clydach, they were abandoned in the 1920s.

Three
Waterfalls

The middle Clynwyn Fall,
Pontneddfechan.

Lime Pool Falls, Pontneddfechan.

Clyn Gwyn Falls, Pontneddfechan.

Upper Cil Hepste Falls, Pontneddfechan.

The falls at Pontneddfechan.

LADY FALL GLYN, NEATH.   Nº 3.

A shroud of water at Lady Falls, Glynneath.

Glancing, dancing falls on the Mellte, in the Vale of Neath.

ON THE MELLTE RIVER, YSTRADFELLTE, Nr MERTHYR-TYDFIL.

58

Aberdulais Falls.

The falls and sluice wheel in the Vale of Neath.

Another view of the falls at Aberdulais.

Four

Working Life

Dyffryn colliery.

Main Colliery No. 7 pit in Skewen was sunk in 1910. The Main Colliery Co. named their pits by numbers and the one illustrated here was approximately 1,000 yards south-east of pits Nos. 3 and 4. No. 8 shaft was located some 140 yards to the east, and served only as an upcast for the colliery. The seams worked from No. 7 pit were the Graigola and Victoria seams, which eventually extended nearly a mile northwards from the shaft. The area was rich with coal and lay between the Dyffryn and Cwmfelin faults. The coal would have been transported by wagons directly to the Neath Abbey wharves. Pits Nos. 7 and 8 stopped work in 1927 and were abandoned in 1928.

Another view of Main Colliery's No. 7 pit, Skewen, *c.* 1905.

The colliery boys and men pose for a photograph with their safety lamps, at Main Colliery, c. 1910. Has the lad seated five from the left a candle holder or billy can at his feet?

A picture of staff at Main Colliery's Nos. 1, 6 and 7 pits, c. 1916. One wonders what was written on the scroll held by the manager, Mr Sam Davies. On the back row, from left to right: Lloyd Samuel, W.M. Lewis, B. Davies, Edward Powell, G. Owen, W.M. Davies, and -?-. On the second row: T.A. Thomas, J.N. Jones, William Thomas, David Richards, J. Davies, J. Richards, L. Williams and T. Howells. Seated: David Williams, J. Bushell, A. Jones, W.H. Jewell, Sam Davies (manager), G.H. Rutter, T. Jones, T. Thomas and F. Davies.

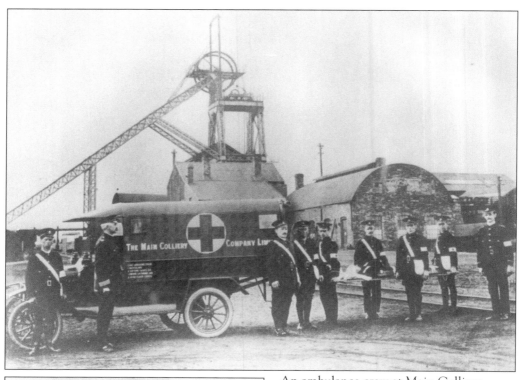

An ambulance crew at Main Colliery, Skewen, *c.* 1905.

The last dram of coal being hauled out of the Darren Colliery, Longford, in 1984. David Fox is the haulier.

The electrical power station of the Main Colliery Company's No. 1 pit, Skewen.

The Main Colliery Company's No. 3 pit, Skewen. This is a view is taken from the screens.

Three men relax on a bank near Main Colliery, Skewen. Unfortunately, their names are not recorded for posterity.

A view of the sidings of No. 1 pit, Skewen.

Colliers of Nos. 3 and 4 pits, Skewen, *c.* 1900.

Four young men and a little girl pose by one of the engines at Main Colliery, Skewen.

A view of Drummau Head, from the Highlands. On the right are Main Colliery's Nos. 3 and 4 pits.

This delightful picture depicts Dynevor Road in the background, which is little changed today. The row of forty houses was built around 1900, mainly for workmen employed by the Main Colliery Company. Dynevor Road is known in some circles as Coronation Road, because its construction coincided with the coronation of Edward VII. A lane at each end of the row gave access to the pits. The lower lane passed the white-washed cottage or farm called Cwrt-y-Clafdy, which was once the infirmary for Neath Abbey. The lane then went through a semi-circular arch under the lower siding of the mine and emerged, briefly, before entering a high rectangular tunnel under the top surface. The path climbed past the colliery pond and ended on Drummau Road. What stories the children in the foreground would have carried with them into old age? A new housing development now stands on the site of the colliery.

Hauliers of Cwrt-y-Bettws colliery, *c.* 1913.

The contentious open cast site, high above Glynneath. This picture was taken in 1981, since then the site has moved right through the hillside.

Cwrt Herbert Colliery, Neath Abbey, was situated on the site of the, now closed, Shell petrol station and was probably developed very near the site of one of the earlier Neath Abbey collieries started by Richard Parsons in 1793. This earlier colliery was worked by Richard Parsons in 1854, but in 1886 he relinquished the mine to the Dynevor Coal Company, who managed it until the Main Colliery Company was formed in 1892. The colliery employed 249 workers in 1895, rising to 371 in 1918, and ceased working in January 1929, when the Main Colliery Company closed down. In its day it was reputed to have been the deepest mine in Europe.

Screening and cleaning belts, Cwrt Herbert Colliery, in 1913. Generally it was the older or partly disabled men and young boys of twelve to fourteen years who were employed to pick out the stone from the run of the mine coal. After the age of fourteen, the boys would usually be transferred underground, as colliers' assistants.

The demolition of the stack at Bryncoch Colliery's No. 1 pit, in 1927. The stack was razed by fire. The five men pictured on the next page worked at the base of the chimney removing bricks, two men inside and three outside. The bricks were then replaced by timbers. Once complete the timber was soaked in paraffin and fired. The chimney fell very quickly.

The men involved in the demolition were, from left to right: Reg Elias, Tom Arnold, John Jenkins, John Tredwell and Tommy Evans. When he was well into his eighties, and just before he died, Reg Elias told us that seconds after they fired the stack and were walking back to the paraffin shed, the chimney fell behind them. They ran and were lucky to escape with their lives.

Workers at the Metalclad Ltd engineering works, in 1937.

Workers at the Melin Tinplate works, *c.* 1916.

Cardonnel tinplate works, Skewen, *c.* 1890. The site was between the Tennant Canal and the Vale of Neath railway, thus ensuring easy access for both incoming and outgoing materials. The business was owned by the Rosser family of Cilfrew.

Aberdulais Tinworks was originally established in Ynysygerwn, but later transferred to Aberdulais. The works ceased operations in the 1930s.

The remains of a blast furnace, at Neath Abbey ironworks, taken in the 1960s. This ironworks was the best known in the area, with evidence of operations, in the late eighteenth century, by the entrepreneur Richard Parsons in the area called Cwmfelin. Towards the end of the eighteenth century, Parson leased the works to the Cornish families of Fox and Price, who produced material which was exported throughout the world. The company fostered talented employees too, none less than David Thomas who was born in Tyllwyd Farm, Wernduu, Brynoch. He served his apprenticeship at Neath Abbey, and later went to work in Ynyscedwyn in the Swansea valley. He eventually went to America where he founded the anthracite iron industry.

Heavy industry on the banks of the River Neath. This example was taken in 1951. The main bulk of movement on the river at Briton Ferry now deals in sand, shale and coal.

An aerial picture of the BP works, at Llandarcy, in the 1950s.

A general view of the BP refinery taken from the south, *c.* 1950.

The refinery, taken from the north-north-west, *c.* 1950.

76

Pipe laying, at Skewen, in the 1950s. The disruption caused by the road diggers changes little, although the equipment used today is more compact.

A BP tanker overturned near the Llandarcy roundabout, in the late 1950s. The incident happened at the bottom of Pen-yr-Heol, Skewen.

It was quite a job getting the lorry the correct way up!

Skewen railway station, *c.* 1950. This was Skewen's second station; the first was opposite the Traveller's Well. The station pictured here was near Picton Terrace and was axed by Dr Beeching, in 1957. In the mid 1990s, the third station to operate in Skewen was opened on the Lonlas side of Station Road.

Neath railway station, on the Swansea to London line, *c.* 1900.

Briton Ferry Road station, at Jersey Marine, on the Vale of Neath line to Swansea. Note the tower on the right, which contained a camera obscura.

SEA.200.   THE NEW BRIDGE. BRITON FERRY. NEAR SWANSEA.

The new bridge, Briton Ferry, taken in 1960. The newer bridge crosses the River Neath a little nearer the sea.

An aerial picture of the Neath river bridge under construction at Briton Ferry, *c.* 1950. The roundabout has traffic on it and the first section of the bridge will carry vehicles over the Brunel Dock. The second section crosses the Neath river.

The wharf and tannery, *c.* 1900.

It is possible sometimes to forget that Neath is near the sea, and that this brings with it activities more readily recognised by the more prominent coastal towns. The following pictures depict activities on the River Neath at Neath Abbey and Briton Ferry wharves.

A vessel belonging to the Main Colliery Company.

There is much activity on the River Neath, with this view of the shippingstaiths, *c.* 1910. Also note the Middlesborough registered *Eskwood*.

Wharfage bays, showing Neath in the background, with the Pentrefynnon area of Skewen on the left; Mynydd Drummau oversees the scene, *c.* 1910.

George Gorvett, pictured here with one of his barge horses, *c.* 1930. Among the tasks performed by Mr Gorvett, was bringing children from the isolated Pritchard's Cottages to school at Jersey Marine between 1922 and 1937.

In the 1930s, Allin's grocer's was located on the junction of Wind Street and Water Street. The site is now occupied by Boots the Chemist. The building on the far right of the picture is now used by the Social Services and is little changed.

This picture of the crew members of the Abbey Omnibus Company was taken opposite Ty Mawr, Neath Abbey.

The Abbey Bus Company, in 1930. Some of the drivers and mechanics included in this picture are: Bob Merrick, Dougie Thomas, Mr Clarke, Thomas Ed Davies, Ossie Davies, Len Dawkins, Fred Pascoe, and Will Hopkins.

Bus drivers and conductors are pictured here at the Abbey's depot, which was built on land now occupied by Watt's Tyres. The company ran a service to the outlying villages throughout the town. Note that the destination of the middle bus is Llandarcy.

At one time, charabancs were the norm, and here a party of local shop workers is travelling to one of the popular destinations of the time, Barry or Porthcawl, c. 1920.

This picture shows the Neath Corporation gas tram, close to the Terminus Hotel, Neath Abbey. The Neath and District Tramways Company was formed in 1873, with a line extending from Briton Ferry to Skewen. The trams were originally horse-drawn and the Rector of Neath declared the line open on 19 November 1873. However, in 1896, the company found itself in financial difficulties and was auctioned off and acquired by the Neath Corporation. In 1897, gas trams were purchased from the Blackpool Corporation and these stayed in service until 30 July 1920. The tram track was taken up during the miner's strike of 1921. The maximum speed of the trams was 10mph and on the Neath Abbey gradients, the passengers were often asked to get out and push. Nevertheless, it was always a popular way to travel.

The Richmond Bus Company, *c.* 1920. The driver is unknown, but this picture was found among the papers of Mrs H. White, so perhaps the driver was a relative.

A lovely study of a bus crew, together with a passenger about to embark, *c.* 1920.

This was the first Bluebird coach to be used in Neath. Note the tyres and the uniform that had not yet extended to a peaked hat. Unfortunately, the crew is unknown.

T.W. George & Co. was one of the first companies to engage themselves in the business of moving items by vehicular transport. The company was based in Sidings Terrace, Skewen.

Hay making on the Dyffryn Estate, Brynoch. Neath's prosperity is traditionally said to be based on mining, copper and iron foundries, but the area has also had a large agricultural presence.

Four boys 'help on the hay' at Cwm Clydach in 1939. The are, from left to right: Bill Meredith, Brian Loosemore, Brian Harvey and Alan Harvey.

A threshing machine working at Cefn Saeson Fawr Farm, Cimla, in 1952.

Richard Vaughan Price, on the left, and his brother David Morgan Price, when they were working on the fields of Longford Farm, c. 1950. To the left of the picture is the mineworker's cottage called Bath House which was demolished in the early 1960s. In the background is Mynydd Drummau.

Washing machines were a dream for Mrs Ruth Griffiths, née Hopkins, who is stood on the left, at the Ironworks Cottages, Neath Abbey, in 1920. Also in the picture are Dai Hopkins, Dylan Rees and Mrs Jean Hopkins.

A copy on an unusual licence – one to slaughter animals. It was issued to David John Payne, from Neath Abbey, in 1934. Up to the 1960s, there were two operating slaughter houses in the town, one at Cwrt Herbert and one on Eastland Road.

No. 7

SLAUGHTER OF ANIMALS ACT, 1933.

Licence to Slaughter Animals.

In pursuance of the provisions of the Slaughter of Animals Act, 1933, the

Neath Borough Council

being a Local Authority for purposes of the said Act, do hereby, on the application

of *David John Payne*

of *10, The Croft, Neath Abbey, Neath.*

grant a Licence to the said *David John Payne*

for the period of *three* year [s] from the *first*

day of *January* 1934, to slaughter or stun animals

in a Slaughter-house or Knacker's Yard in accordance with the said Act.

By order of the Local Authority.

Signed *Alfred E. Curtis*
Town Clerk.

Dated this *twenty-seventh* day of *December* 1933.

Copyright. Shaw & Sons Ltd., Fetter Lane, E.C.4. 834s1 (s)

[P.T.O.

91

A pastoral scene of Jersey Marine village, *c.* 1850. This picture illustrates a time when the road was a track and the means of transport, the horse.

June Price of Longford Farm, inside the milk float on Rhydhir, Neath Abbey, in the 1960s. The horse was called Champion and this was probably one of the last horse-drawn floats to deliver milk in the area.

Five

The Church

Neath Abbey, *c.* 1950. The site, used for many religious gatherings, was the most hallowed place in the Neath area. Corpus Christi processions regularly terminated here, and multi-denominational festivals were held in the grounds.

The Archbishop of Wales consecrated an extension to the cemetery of St Matthew's church, Dyffryn, Bryncoch, in the 1950s.

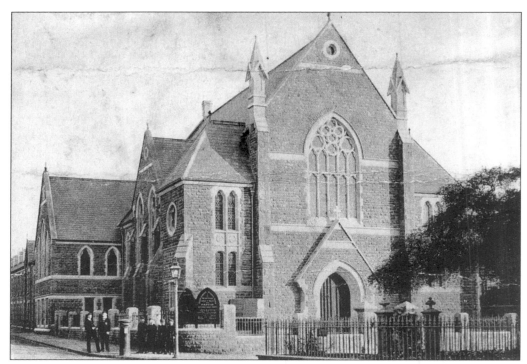

The English Presbyterian church, set on the corner with Greenway Road and London Road, in Neath, *c.* 1930.

St Illtyd's church, Llantwit, Neath.

An unusual scene, taken from the Drummau mountains in 1980. The Salvation Army can be seen celebrating Easter with an outdoor service. This was an annual event for a number years, until vandals rudely damaged the cross.

Wesley chapel, Neath Abbey, *c.* 1980.

St Catwg's church, Cadoxton, near Neath, *c.* 1900.

The inhabitants of Neath are pictured here, following the Cross through the streets, in the 1920s.

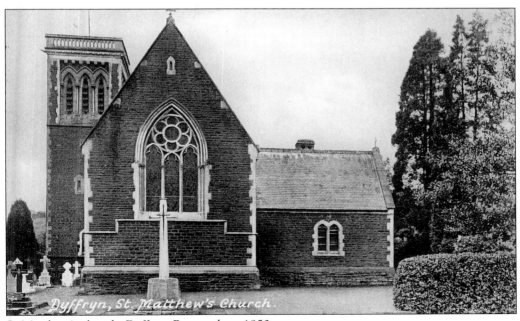

St Matthew's church, Dyffryn, Bryncoch, c. 1950.

The interior of St Matthew's church, *c.* 1950.

The choir of St Matthews church, Dyffryn, Bryncoch, in 1920. On the back row, from left to right: Harry Gosling, William Gosling, Earnest Gosling, Eddie Jones, and David Tremayne. On the second row: William Tremayne, -?-, Tom Harris, Arthur Jones, and Harold Bradley. On the third row: Walter Adams, Tom Jones, Jeff Jenkins, Willie Jones, Willie McCutcheon, Oswald Davies, Idris Gosling, and Edmond Thomas. On the fourth row: Edgar McCutcheon, Harry Burton, Albert Bailey, -?-, Reg Cooke, Les Edwards, -?-, Worthington Thomas, Trevor Tremayne, Jackie Bowen, Ivor Edwards, and W. Bendle. Seated: A.R. Davies (curate), J.C. Thomas (vicar), David Lewis (choir master), and Joseph Thomas (organist).

Jubilee celebrations at St Matthew's church, Dyffryn, Bryncoch, on 21 September 1921. On the back row, from left to right: Mr Thomas, Joseph Thomas, Mr Duncan, Jack Evans, Tom Harris, Bill Tremayne, Mr Harris, Mr Bradley, Colonel Gwyn, -?-, Mr Davies (curate), Mr Duncan, and Tom Evans. Seated: Mrs Edith Moore-Gwyn, Mr Theodore Gibbins, J.C. Thomas (vicar), Joseph Edward Moore-Gwyn, Howell Joseph Moore-Gwyn, and Mrs Margaret Laura Thomas (the vicar's wife).

St Thomas' church, Neath, c. 1910.

Aberpergwm church, Glynneath, *c.* 1900.

A certificate presented to Miss Catherine Beasley, *c.* 1920. The Band of Hope was a temperance movement, usually run and organised by the Sunday schools. There would be weekly meetings for children, who would enjoy a variety of activities. However, unlike Sunday school, the accent was always on an anti-alcohol theme. This certificate shows 'Illustrious War Abstainers' and was awarded through the Skewen lower school (Ysgol Mynachlog Nedd) to Catherine for the manner in which she reported a lecture on the nature and effects of alcohol – not alcohol abuse, you notice. To the Band of Hope movement, the partaking of any alcohol was abusive.

St John's church, Skewen, in the 1950s. Note the vicarage to the left.

The Revd Alfred Richard Davies, pictured with his bible class in 1925, outside the Dyffryn vicarage, now called Swiss Gables. On the back row, from left to right: Miss Reynolds, Mrs Eistedd, Mrs Jones, Mrs Lewis, Nurse Lilian Garland, Mrs William Tremayne, Mrs Corbett, Mrs Evans, Mrs Fowler, Mrs James, Mrs Davies, Mrs Davies, Mrs Eccles, and Mrs Davies. On the second row: Mrs Morgans, Mrs Tom Tremayne, Mrs Bunn, Mrs Adams, Mrs Harris, Mrs Samson, Mrs Evans, Mrs Evans, Mrs Prosser, Mrs Trebble, Mrs Jones, Mrs Jones and Mrs Hale. On the front row: Mrs Jones, Mrs Prout, Mrs Edwards, Mrs Mary Bowen, Mrs Gwen Jenkins, Revd Alfred Richard Davies, Mrs Stanway, Mrs Taylor, Miss Ace and Mrs Howells.

The Vaughan Tower of St David's church, Neath, taken from Victoria Gardens, *c*. 1970.

Ebenezer chapel choir, Neath Abbey, in 1949.

Member of the Sunday school at Ebenezer chapel, Neath Abbey, in 1905.

Like all chapels in the pre-war period, the members of Moriah, Taillwyd Road chapel were very socially active. This picture shows their cricket team in 1914. On the back row, from left to right: James Mayrick, and Billy Griffiths. On the second row: Tom Jones, Dai Fowler, Jim Mayrick, Tom Griffiths, Mr Phillips, Bill Davies, C. Hopkins, Mr Duncan, and G. Rewbridge. On the third row, seated: Arthur Griffiths, Will Griffiths, Mr Prosser, and -?-. On the front row: David Abraham, -?-, James Elias Jones, -?-, and Thomas G. Meyrick. The boy on the left at the front is B. Rewbridge. The boy on the right in unknown.

Six

Sport and Leisure

The focus of this picture is not the ruins of Neath Abbey in the foreground, but the buildings on the left. They were used to compliment the Neath Dragons speedway stadium, c. 1960. The track was red ash and about a quarter of a mile around. Stock car racing preceded the motor bikes. Despite attracting huge crowds, Speedway proved, in a short time, to be a financial failure and closed down forever. A prefabricated buildings company called Swiftplan now occupies the site.

NEATH ABBEY
Speedway

PROVINCIAL LEAGUE CHAMPIONSHIP
Sponsored by the makers of Senior Service Cigarettes

WELSH DRAGONS
v.
MIDDLESBROUGH BEARS

SATURDAY, 18th AUGUST, 1962
at 7 p.m.

PROGRAMME - - - - 6D.

A rare copy of the Neath (Welsh) Dragons Speedway team programme. Middlesborough Bears did not beat the Dragons in this meeting, in August 1962 in Neath Abbey and they soon took flight from the shadow of the Abbey. Note that the league was sponsored by a tobacco company. Along with rugby, Speedway was the sport that carried the town's name in the national newspapers on a weekly basis. They were highly successful as a racing outfit, but not so as a commercial venture.

Sports day at Rhydhir school, *c.* 1960. The events were usually competed for in teams which were called Houses; this is the same system used to stage the Eisteddfod competitions. They were always hotly contested affairs, with team loyalties crossing friendships in the most sporting of manners.

Horse racing on the Drummau Mountain, *c.* 1970. This is a picture of the horse Pine B, with its jockey, Waine Foster jumping the last fence in the members' race. Horse racing has taken place periodically in several locations in Neath: for instance, at the Skewen dog track, Tennant Park and at Cefn Saeson in Cimla. There has also been unrecognised flat racing at Pentreclywda and Cwmgwrach, and a very successful point-to-point steeplechase course existed in the early 1990s at Rheola, which was built by the Banwen Miners' Hunt. At the turn of the century, recognised flat racing took place on the Burrows at Jersey Marine and the races are recorded in the annals of the Jockey Club. Unfortunately, no horse racing takes place within the boundaries of the Neath area today.

Horses are being lead away after their race at Rheola Racecourse, in the Vale of Neath, in 1992.

A picture of the Glynfelin hounds. The Master of the Hunt was Theodore Gibbins. He was an industrialist and agriculturalist and for about thirty years, was managing director of the Melin Tinplate Company. Several members of this Quaker family were notable captains of industry in the area. For a period of twenty-five years Theodore Gibbins was a member of the executive committee of the Welsh Plate and Sheet Manufactures' Association. He also served on the employers' side of the industry's Joint Industrial Council. He acted as High Sheriff of Glamorgan from 1928/9, was a Justice of the Peace, and a member of Neath borough council, where he chaired the finance committee. He was a member of the governing body of the Church in Wales, and was also chairman of the Llandaf Board of Finance. He was a member of St Matthew's church, Dyffryn, and a Knight of the Venerable Order of St John. In addition to these activities, he was president of the Neath Conservative and Unionist Association, and served as chairman of the now defunct Neath and District Agricultural Society. He served terms as president of both Neath Antiquarian Society and Neath cricket club, and was treasurer of the Welsh Boy Scouts' Association. During the Great War he was Commandant of the 83rd detachment of the Glamorgan Voluntary Aid. He was also the employers' representative of the Glamorgan Territorial Force Association. This picture, taken at Glynfelin in Hound Field, shows Mr Gibbins in the centre, and to his right is Mr James Hicks. The gentleman on his left is unknown. The pack hunted the Drummau for hare and fox.

The traditional Boxing Day meet of the Banwen Miners' Hunt outside the Castle Hotel, on the Parade, Neath. This meet has been held since the early 1960s. The rider nearest the hotel is the Master of the Hunt, Billy Hancock.

Young members of the Skewen St John's Ambulance Brigade pose for this photograph, c. 1959. The officer is Mr Bowen from Villiers Road, Skewen. This picture was taken outside Cowbridge, on the way home from a rally in Cardiff.

A delightful picture of Skewen Lower Brownies, in 1972. This picture was taken during a presentation made by the group to Mr Thomas of Rhydhir, who was one of the first people in the Neath area to be guided by a dog trained to lead the blind. Making the presentation to Mr Thomas is Mrs Gwen Slee, the Brownies' leader who lived in Brookville Drive, Skewen.

The pupils and staff of Mynachlog Nedd school celebrate the Jubilee, in the 1930s.

Members of the Skewen and Neath Abbey Co-operative Society's going on their annual outing, in 1929. Note the pull down open windows on the bus.

The Neath Antiquarian Society entertain members of the Cambrian Archaeological Association with tea and candlelight in the sub dortor at Neath Abbey, in the 1920s.

These are two pictures of the refreshment sheds at Jersey Marine beach, seen in the 1920s. Bathing costumes could be hired, cycles stored, and parties would be catered for. The village was a popular seaside resort in the late nineteenth century and although not quite as busy as Blackpool, it certainly provided the summer focus for Neath and the valleys.

A picture taken at Dyffryn Clydach, in 1939. From left to right, Brian Loosmore, Alan Harvey (at the back), Brian Harvey and Teddy Davy.

Mrs Evelyn Price of Longford Farm, with two of her eight children, Cyril and June Price, in the 1930s.

Two men and a boy who came from the Penyard area of Neath, *c. 1930*. What is in the jars held with wire or string? They are, from left to right: Alfred Roch, Wilfred John and Jenkin John.

Mr Morgan Price and his wife Hannah Jane Price, of Cwrt Herbert with their two daughters Olwen, on the left, and Betty, known as Little Betty, on the right. This picture was taken on the occasion of Betty's marriage to Gwyn Maybery, *c. 1930*.

The Festival of Britain was celebrated in Charles Street, Skewen, in 1951.

The Festival of Britain was also celebrated in Penyard, in 1951.

They were celebrating the Festival of Britain on Longford Road too. Included in the picture are: Mrs John, Mrs D. Williams, Mrs Greenaway, Mrs Worth, J. Good, Mrs Good, Mrs Morgan, Mrs Venables, Mrs Vibart, Peter Venables, Marshall David, Victor Morgan, Kathleen Worth, Margaret Greenaway, Barbara Greenaway and Audrey Worth.

Seven

Wartime

"NEATH'S WAR MEMORIAL GATES". *PHOTO HARRY JONES. NEATH.*

Neath's war memorial gates were sited at the entrance to the Gnoll grounds, *c.* 1937.

The Neath Abbey Comforts Fund

1939–1945

Registered under the War Charities' Act, 1940

Left: A part of a foreign field will always be Wales. Neath soldier Cyril Vines Payne, who came from the Abbey, was killed on active service in Tunis on the 8 November 1943, aged 36.

Right: A copy of the souvenir card made for the Neath Abbey Comforts Funds. This group was formed in 1939 to obtain funds for the purchase of gifts to send to local servicemen and women. House to house collections were made on a weekly basis, and in addition, the committee arranged fund raising events such as concerts, dances, and whist drives. The fund received strong support from the community. Postal orders were sent to every serving member from the village, until the end of the war, when collections ceased on VJ Day in August 1945. The deposit of the fund was closed and shared out between the 277 personnel who had served in the forces from Dyffryn Clydach. As a matter of record, of the 277 people who served their country, six became prisoners of war and eight made the supreme sacrifice.

The Stretcher Bearers Unit attached to the Neath Abbey Home Guard defended the home front, c. 1940.

These two pictures of Neath's thriving Home Guard platoon were taken near the Cwrt Herbert Barracks.

Presented by

THE
BLAENHONDDAN
PARISH COUNCIL

in commemoration of attendance at a

VICTORY TEA

held at the

CADOXTON and BRYNCOCH
SCHOOLS

On Thursday, September 6, 1945

as a memento of

V-E and V-J DAYS,
May 7th and August 15th, 1945

which marked

THE END OF A GREAT WORLD CONFLICT.

Blaenhonddan parish council published this pamphlet as a momento to VE and VJ days. It was used to launch a Victory Tea which was held at the Cadoxton and Bryncoch schools on Thursday 15 September 1945.

The children celebrate at Bryncoch, spilling out onto the main road. However, traffic would have been lighter in 1945; if any cars had passed, the occupants would probably have joined in, such was the occasion.

Eight
Life and Times

This picture emphasises what might have been, for the literature in the Vale of Neath. This picture of Robert Southey was painted around 1807. A few years before this, the poet had come close to finalising an arrangement with Squire Williams, the owner of Maesgwyn, in Neath, for the tenancy of the property. However, it all came to nothing, and Southey decided to live in Keswick. Ironically, the Robert Southey Society, which was set up in 1985, is based at Abergarwed, a few miles down the road from Maesgywn.

MARTHA YOUNG
DIED 29TH OF 8TH MONTH
1847 AGED 78.
WILLIAM WESTON YOUNG
DIED 24TH OF 8TH MONTH
1866 AGED 68.
MARY YOUNG
DIED 5TH OF 4TH MONTH
1867 AGED 63.

This is the headstone of the artist William Weston Young in the Quaker's graveyard, on James Street. Young gave us many fine sketches and paintings reflecting scenes on the area, together with a fine book, *Guide to the Scenery of Glynneath*. His reference to Glynneath means the Vale of Neath was not yet the modern village. Young died in 1847, in Kidderminster.

Howel Cuthbertson Esq, a member of Neath's high society, who resided at the delightful Darren Court. He served as Mayor of the town during 1869/70, and before that, he was a coroner for Glamorgan in 1864.

This picture shows the front of the political pamphlet of S.T. Evans, a respected Liberal who hailed from Skewen. He contested the Mid-Glamorgan seat in the 1892 General Election and won.

MID-GLAMORGAN ELECTION, 1892.

S. T. EVANS,
THE LIBERAL CANDIDATE.

Printed and Published by W. Jones, The (WJ) Factory, off Golden Lane, E.C.

A debonair gent, Mr Hywel Walter Kirkhouse, is pictured here outside Darren Court, in 1893. He was a notable engineer, and was involved in many projects in the area, including the building of the Tennant canal.

Mr Henry Bradley was the head gardener at Dyffryn House, and is standing here with his prized hydrangea. Fêtes and flower shows were held in the grounds of Dyffryn House, and marquees would be erected in front of the mansion. Mr Bradley was a frequent winner and was often commended on the beauty of his floral displays in church on festive occasions.

Upstairs at the big house was grand but downstairs had dignity. The staff of Dyffryn House are pictured under the arch of the stable block.

Another picture of Dyffryn staff. Note the young man second from the left wearing goggles, an early driver perhaps? Note the elaborate collared livery of the man on the left. Sitting in the centre with the sterness of authority is the butler who ruled below stairs.

The coach and horses still await, but time does not. This picture, taken outside the coachouse, Dyffryn Mansion has coachman William Adams, waiting for instructions to convey the Gwyn's or their guests to a function, in the 1880s.

The coachman, William Adams as a young man, riding a cob at the Dyffryn stables, *c.* 1870.

This is the front cover of the programme of services which was held outside Joseph Tregelles Price's house, Ty Mawr, in Neath Abbey. It commemorated the unveiling of a plaque to his memory. J.T. Price was a local industrialist, and philanthropist and was one of the founders of the International Peace Society, which was the forerunner of the League of Nations. The League of Nations lead to what we know today as the United Nations. Price was a true internationalist, who despised violence. Despite the attractions of a lucrative market, he steadfastly refused to produce armaments of any kind at his Neath Abbey ironworks. He also petitioned the Home Secretary and the King of England, to seek a reprieve for the first Welsh working class martyr, Dic Penderyn. Price is buried in the Quaker's graveyard, in James Street, Neath.

A picture of the Neath valley poet, Chris Torrance, taken in 1975. He lives in an isolated cottage between Pontneddfechan and Ystradfellta and is the author of a number of books, many of which reflect life in the valley.

An overview, seeing most of Neath from Briton Ferry. Drummau Mountain is on the left and the dome top of Mynydd March Hywel is on the right.